CLEVELAND, OHIO

A PHOTOGRAPHIC PORTRAIT

PHOTOGRAPHS BY
CARL STIMAC

NARRATIVE BY
NANCY LOYAN SCHUEMANN

First published in the United States of
America by:

Twin Lights Publishers, Inc.
8 Hale Street
Rockport, Massachusetts 01966
Telephone: (978) 546-7398
http://www.twinlightspub.com

ISBN: 1-885435-86-X
ISBN: 978-1-885435-86-6

Jacket back:
Baltimore & Ohio Railroad Bridge

Jacket front and opposite:
Cleveland skyline from the Northeast side of the city

Frontispiece:
Conrail Bridge or "Iron Curtain Bridge"

Book design by:
LJ Lindhurst
www.w-rabbit.com

Printed in China

INTRODUCTION

When General Moses Cleaveland, selected by the Connecticut Land Company to open the Western Reserve territory to colonization, landed where the Cuyahoga River meets Lake Erie on July 22, 1796, little did he imagine a vibrant metropolis with a glittering skyline. Though Cleaveland planned on naming the village after the river, his associates convinced him to name the village after himself.

Through the years, the "a" was dropped and the farming village grew into the City of Cleveland. With the construction of the Ohio Canal in the 1820s, the creation of railroads and roads, and the use of steamships, commerce, and trade established an industrial base that continued to flourish.

During the Industrial Age, the iron ore, petroleum, and steel industries created prosperity and millionaires like John D. Rockefeller. Euclid Avenue became the "Millionaire's Row" where elaborate mansions were erected. Educational, cultural, and medical institutions were founded. Many of the institutions remain such as The Cleveland Museum of Art, Severance Hall, The Cleveland Clinic Foundation, and Case Western Reserve University.

Immigrants arriving in search of work as well as freed slaves created neighborhoods of ethnic diversity. Their influence continues in the shops and restaurants that thrive in the city and its suburbs, from Ohio City to Chinatown.

Industry has given way to technology and health care has become the city's dominant business, with The Cleveland Clinic Foundation as the city's largest employer.

Education is at the forefront with major institutions of higher learning such as Case Western Reserve University and Medical School, Cleveland State University, The Cleveland Institute of Art, and Cuyahoga Community College located in the central city. Culture abounds with the museums in University Circle and on the lakefront, the Theater District at Playhouse Square, the Cleveland Playhouse, the renowned Cleveland Orchestra at Severance Hall, and the Rock and Roll Hall of Fame and Museum. Sports thrill with the winning Cleveland Indians, Cleveland Browns, Cleveland Cavaliers, Cleveland City Stars, and Lake Erie Monsters.

Like most major urban cities of the Midwest, Cleveland has continued to reinvent itself and thrive. This is evident in the variety of architectural styles of its buildings from Neo-Classical to I.M. Pei. From its roots as an industrial city to the "New Urbanism," Cleveland is undergoing a transformation. New downtown neighborhoods are being created in the once industrial Flats, the Warehouse District, East Fourth Street, the Avenue District, Euclid Avenue, and University Circle.

Cleveland, Ohio: A Photographic Portrait is a glimpse into the places, events, and people that make this jewel on the shores of Lake Erie a unique place to visit and explore.

Experience Cleveland through the lens of local photographer Carl Stimac as he takes you on a visual journey to the landmarks, historical sites, gardens, entertainment venues, and events that make this city great.

History Meets Technology *(opposite)*

The landmark copper-domed clock tower of the historic West Side Market at West 25th and Lorain Avenue stands as a reminder of Cleveland's storied past. The 137-foot tower, originally a water tower, has withstood the passage of time as Voss Aerospace, a high-tech firm, represents the future.

Sentinel on the Lake

The city's skyline as viewed from North Coast Harbor is reflective of its distinct architecture. The Rock and Roll Hall of Fame and Museum and Great Lakes Science Center are at the forefront while Key Tower dwarfs the British Petroleum Building and historic Terminal Tower. When constructed in 1930, the Terminal Tower was the tallest building in the world outside of New York City. Key Tower, built in 1991, exceeds it in height by five stories.

Cleveland has been known as the "Rock and Roll" capital of the country ever since local disc jockey Alan Freed coined the term in the 1950s. Renowned architect I.M. Pei of Pei Cobb Freed and Partners, New York City, designed the Rock and Roll Hall of Fame and Museum, opened in 1995, as a tribute to music and musicians.

City on the Lake *(opposite, top)*

Looking northwest, the sun sets over Lake
Erie and downtown Cleveland. The skyline is
aglow as buildings light up at dusk.

City of Bridges *(opposite, bottom)*

Cleveland has been called a "City of Bridges."
The city is split in half by the serpentine
Cuyahoga River. East and West sides are connected by high-level spans, movable bridges,
and lengthy train crossings. Constructed over
uneven terrain and industrial sites, bridges
lead to and from downtown.

Winter's Eve *(above)*

Holiday lights ignite Public Square. The
annual lighting ceremony, held the day after
Thanksgiving, draws thousands and features
an antique carriage parade, entertainment,
and a multitude of festive lights that remain
lit throughout the holiday season.

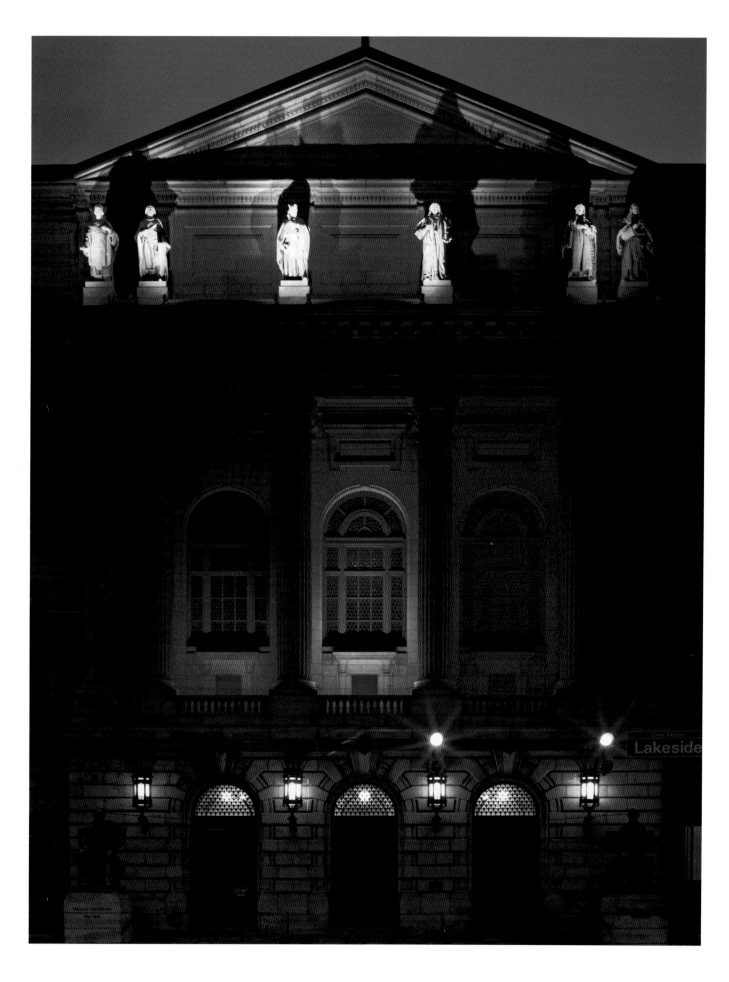

Seat of Power *(above)*

Rich wood detailing, a carved marble fire-place, classical design, and rich bold fabric add a sense of power, yet a touch of intimacy to the multifunctional suite, serving as the of-ficial business office for the mayor of the city of Cleveland.

Order in the Court *(right)*

Constructed in 1910, renovated and renamed in 2005, the Howard M. Metzenbaum United States Courthouse features a façade of granite and stately bronze doors.

Hall of Government *(opposite)*

Cleveland City Hall, dedicated on July 4, 1916, was the first hall built for and owned by the city. The arcaded ground story, two-story colonnade, and central entrance bay are characteristic of the Beaux-Arts style. Outdoor illumination, added during the 1970s renova-tion, highlights the exterior's Vermont granite.

Cuyahoga County Courthouse *(above)*

The courthouse maintains its historical court-rooms with original incandescent chandeliers, wall sconces, rich woodwork, and canvas murals. Four additional courtrooms are in this hall of justice.

Corridors of Power *(left)*

Spacious corridors in the courthouse feature original elegant marble walls and arches, high ornamental plaster ceilings, skylights, stone floors, and mahogany doors and frames.

National City Bank *(opposite)*

The oldest bank in the city, incorporated in 1845 as the City Bank of Cleveland, National City Bank's main building on Euclid Avenue is a fine example of Beaux-Arts design. A double colonnade of fluted columns, support-ing an ornate coffered ceiling, towers over the pink marble-clad banking room.

FEDERAL RESERVE BANK OF CLEVELAND

FEDERAL RESERVE BANK

Banking on Cleveland *(above)*

Cleveland was named one of the districts of the Federal Reserve in 1913. Conceived by bankers and designed by noted Cleveland architects Walker and Weeks in 1923, the 12-story Federal Reserve Bank of Cleveland is modeled after Michelozzo's *Medici-Riccardi Palace* in Florence, Italy, home of bankers of the Renaissance. With a pink granite base, the upper stories are faced with pinkish marble, and elaborate iron grilles that accent windows.

Artist's Touch *(left)*

Two freestanding statues, *Commerce and Jurisprudence*, created by Chester French in 1911, flank the arched main entrance of the Federal Reserve Bank of Cleveland.

Brush Arc Lamp *(opposite)*

A foliated wrought-iron post supporting an acorn-style basket light fixture adorns the southwest corner of the historic Society for Savings Building on Public Square. It is a fine example of inventor Charles Brush's arc light. Cleveland was the first city in the nation to light its streets exclusively by electricity.

The Cleveland Orchestra on Public Square

A summer tradition, the internationally
renowned Cleveland Orchestra, founded in
1918, leaves its home in stately Severance
Hall in University Circle to perform in a
larger, more public venue without charge.
Here, the orchestra and music director Franz
Welser-Möst perform in the 18th annual Star-
Spangled Spectacular and Festival.

Human Concerto

Crowds gather early in front of the Tower City complex on Public Square to spend a summer's evening of classical music under the stars. The Cleveland Orchestra concert culminates in a bursting display of fireworks.

Cleveland Public Library *(opposite, top)*

The library's main building of classic Beaux-Arts design was the result of a competition won by architects Walker and Weeks. It features a rusticated arch base, balustrade roofline, and a three-story Corinthian colonnade. The library system is one of the largest public libraries in the country.

Lending Department *(opposite, bottom)*

In 1999, the main building of the Cleveland Public Library underwent a major restoration and construction of the new Louis Stokes Wing. The Lending Department / Atrium, also called "The Golden Game", is the entrance to the Wing's collections in business, social sciences, science, and history.

Brett Hall *(above)*

The three-story reading room in the main building of the Cleveland Public Library features a painted vaulted ceiling of Classical design. Custom hand-loomed carpeting, installed during the 1999 renovation, reflects the ceiling motif. The Travertine marble floor and interior design is said to be reminiscent of an ancient Roman bath.

North Point Tower   *(above)*

The tower, constructed in 1985, is a 19-story office building with articulated walls of tile, brick, and silver and green glass. A seven-story wing, added in 1999, is connected by a nine-story angled glass atrium with sweeping views of the city and waterfront.

Carl B. Stokes Federal Courthouse   *(left)*

The curved façade of the new 2002 Carl B. Stokes Federal Courthouse faces the Cuyahoga River and is connected to the Avenue of Tower City complex by an indoor walkway. Designed by architect Arnold W. Brunner, the building is named after the first African-American mayor of a major city.

Top of the Tower   *(opposite)*

A reflective metal pyramid and spire caps off Key Tower, the tallest building in Cleveland and the tallest office building between New York and Chicago. Designed by renowned architect Cesar Pelli and Associates, the 57-story, 888-foot structure is part of Key Center. The complex consists of the Tower, Marriott Hotel, a parking garage, and the historic Society for Savings Building.

Flats, West Bank

Most of the movable bridges over the winding Cuyahoga River were built as part of a 1946 Corp of Engineers project. Visible are a vertical-lift bridge, the Center Street Swing Bridge, and the high-level Veterans Memorial Bridge. All were permanently illuminated in celebration of Cleveland's Bicentennial by lighting designer, Ross De Alessi.

At dusk, the Plain Dealer Pavilion, an outdoor entertainment venue, glows next to the old Powerhouse. Built in 1892 as a streetcar powerhouse, the restored brick landmark with distinctive 240-foot chimneys houses restaurants and nightclubs as part of the Nautica Complex. In the background, Stonebridge Condominiums offer upscale living with views of the river and city.

Over the River

The Veterans Memorial Bridge, the oldest high-level bridge in daily use, straddles the Cuyahoga River. Visible are the Scherzer rolling lift bridge and the famous Center Street Swing Bridge. The swing bridge is the only one in the area and marks the approximate spot where Moses Cleaveland landed.

Homage to Transportation

Serving as gateways to Cleveland's east and west sides, two pairs of giant art deco pylons tower over the Hope Memorial Bridge. Carved of local Berea sandstone, the figures hold a hay rake, covered wagon, stage coach and automobile, symbolizing the progress of transportation. Formerly the Lorain Carnegie Bridge, the roadway was renamed after restoration in the 1980s in honor of Clevelander/entertainer Bob Hope's father, who helped construct it.

Resting Place of John D. Rockefeller
(opposite)

The tallest monument in scenic Lake View Cemetery is the obelisk of John D. Rockefeller, who made his fortune in Cleveland as founder of The Standard Oil Company in 1870. He resided on Euclid Avenue's "Millionaire's Row" and had an estate in Forest Hills before relocating to New York City. He rests eternally with other notables interred in the historic burial ground.

Autumn in Lake View   *(above)*

Known as Cleveland's "outdoor museum," Lake View Cemetery features architectural landmarks from ornately carved headstones and iron-gated family mausoleums, to President Garfield's elaborate tomb and the Jeptha Wade Memorial Chapel. Founded in 1869 as a Victorian garden cemetery, it covers 285 acres of hilly terrain featuring over 500 species of trees. In the spring, over 100,000 daffodils burst into bloom.

The Goodtime III

Docked at the East 9th Street Pier near the
Rock and Roll Hall of Fame and Museum, the
Goodtime III is a family-owned business that
has had the tradition of sailing the Cuyahoga
River since *Goodtime II* operated in 1958. The
current 1,000- passenger luxury ship was com-
pleted in 1990 and offers regular sightseeing
tours of Lake Erie and the Cuyahoga River.

Good Times Ahead   *(top and bottom)*

The *Goodtime III*, Cleveland's largest excursion ship, takes passengers on the "Cuyahoga River Tour." A staple of school field trips, the trip is the city's top sightseeing tour for residents, tourists, and visiting celebrities.

On Deck   *(above and right)*

A scenic view of downtown Cleveland can be seen from the Edgewater Yacht Club. Founded in 1914, the nonprofit organization promotes the sport of boating, a popular Cleveland past time. A diverse group of members gather to enjoy the fun of watercraft and socializing in a relaxed clubhouse atmosphere.

Smooth Sailing   *(opposite)*

The visiting *Appledore V* is moored at North Coast Harbor, located on Lake Erie. Today, the schooner is used primarily for overnight voyaging all over the Great Lakes and offers hands-on science programs for elementary through high school students.

31

The Rock and Roll Hall of Fame and Museum (above)

Geometric curves and angles distinguish this structure as a local landmark. Located at the corner of the entrance to North Coast Harbor, the "Rock Hall" offers interactive exhibits, memorabilia, traveling shows, concerts, and a gift shop. Each year a new group of artists are inducted into the exclusive Hall of Fame located in the building.

Guitar Mania (left)

A collection of ten-foot-high fiberglass replicas of Fender Stratocaster guitars line Key Plaza, gateway to the Rock and Roll Hall of Fame and Museum. Begun in 2002, this public art project features guitars designed by celebrities and local artists and are sponsored by local organizations and businesses. Exhibited on city streets, the guitars arrive at the "Rock Hall" where they are displayed and auctioned off for charity.

"Time" (opposite)

The fiberglass guitar *Time*, by artist Irene Serkle is one of the 100 oversized guitars in the Guitar Mania art exhibit.

The House of Blues *(above and left)*

On Euclid Avenue at the East 4th Street Entertainment District, the House of Blues offers music, dining, a Gospel brunch, and a company store. In addition, it features an Indian-inspired Foundation Room where members enjoy an elegant space for entertainment, dining, and meditation.

Blues Goes Country

Touring artists like Ted Riser and the Marshall Band, presenting country and Southern rock, perform at the House of Blues where the music can be anything from heavy metal to rock and roll to the blues.

East 4th Street Entertainment District

In the historic Gateway neighborhood, East 4th Street has reinvented itself as one of Cleveland's most diverse and popular entertainment destinations. The Pickwick & Frolic Restaurant and Club complex, opened in 2002, includes a 27,000 square-foot bar, a full-service restaurant, a cabaret, martini bar, and the Hilarities 4th Street Theatre. Outdoor dining adds to the festive streetscape.

Hard Rock Cafe

Cleveland's rock 'n' roll tradition makes it the perfect home for Hard Rock Cafe and it's 50 foot neon Fender Stratocaster. Located in Tower City Center, the Cleveland edition of the famous chain carries on the tradition of casual food and rock memorabilia. The chain began as an American diner in London and became famous when musician Eric Clapton gifted the owners with a guitar. Soon, other guitars were added to the collection and other locations opened worldwide.

Fire Food & Drink   *(above)*

Fine restaurants offering international cuisine, specialty shops, offices, rail and bus lines, and a village green make Shaker Square a popular East Side destination. One of the earliest planned shopping centers in the nation and the oldest shopping district in Ohio, the 1929 vintage Square maintains its upscale ambiance and Georgian-style architecture.

Fire!   *(right)*

A chef at one of Shaker Square's fine restaurants, Fire Food & Drink, puts on a light show in the kitchen as he prepares a flaming dish.

Warehouse District   *(opposite)*

On a summer evening, the Warehouse District comes to life with al fresco dining and entertainment. This thriving community of offices, residences, and restaurants around West 3rd Street consists of rehabilitated Italianate, Romanesque, and Eastlake-inspired buildings. Through the 19th Century the district was the commercial center of Cleveland.

The Distillery *(left)*

The Great Lakes Brewing Company is the premier craft brewery in the Great Lakes Region and is located in a neighborhood that was once the heart of Cleveland's brewing industry. Founded by brothers Patrick and Daniel Conway in 1988, it was the first microbrewery in Ohio. Only the freshest ingredients are used without preservatives or pasteurization. The distillery is a 75-300 barrel system.

The Brewpub *(below)*

On tap are the Great Lakes Brewing Company's beers and ales named after famous Cleveland landmarks and citizens. Two Victorian-vintage buildings, one an old tavern, were merged to create the Brewpub. The Taproom retains its 1930s charm with a tiger mahogany bar, Cleveland's oldest. The wood retains bullet holes said to have come from the gun of famous Clevelander, Eliot Ness.

Cleveland City Stars

Professional soccer returned to Cleveland in 2006 with the founding of the Cleveland City Stars, part of the United Soccer League. With Crocodinho as their mascot and a legion of fans called, "The Green Army," the team plays home games at Krenzler Stadium on the campus of Cleveland State University and also sponsors youth soccer programs and camps.

Edgewater Park

Cyclists grace the foreground of Cleveland's skyline as they ride in the Edgewater area of the Cleveland Lakefront State Park. Edgewater Park, located west of the Cuyahoga River, was created in 1894 and continues to attract tourists and residents with bath houses, pavilions, baseball diamonds, playgrounds, picnic areas, and a sandy beach.

Rowing on the River

Members of the Cleveland Rowing Foundation glide across the Cuyahoga River. The Foundation operates the only boathouse in Northeast Ohio. Around 800 adults and youth row on the river from March through November and work as community partners to maintain recreational quality on the Cuyahoga, a river the Mohawk Indians named, meaning, "crooked river."

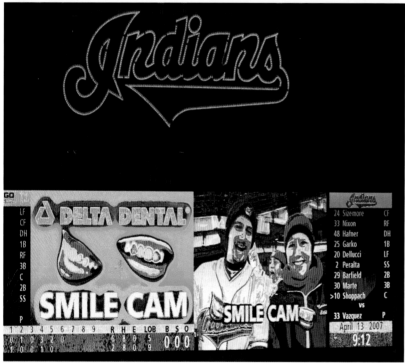

Play Ball *(top)*

Professional baseball is one of Cleveland's oldest traditions, dating back to the 1900s. Progressive Field, formerly Jacobs Field, opened in 1994 and is home of the Cleveland Indians. An intimate park with unobstructed sight lines and angled seating, the stadium was designed for the enjoyment of baseball.

Scoreboard *(bottom)*

When Progressive Field opened, the Daktronics scoreboard was the world's largest baseball video screen. In 2004, on the Field's tenth anniversary, a new system was installed with a giant video screen, 14.9-feet long and 36-feet high with three million LED lights.

Progressive Field, Formerly Jacobs Field

Part of the Gateway Sports and Entertainment Complex, Progressive Field's unclad metal exterior is said to reflect the design of the famed bridges on the Cuyahoga River. The structure's irregular form, numerous levels, open structural elements, and unique vertical light towers create a contemporary presence.

Quicken Loans Arena

In 1994, sports and entertainment returned to downtown Cleveland with the simultaneous completion of Progressive Field (formerly Jacobs Field), the Quicken Loans Arena, and a plaza, thus comprising the Gateway Sports and Entertainment Complex. The 750,000 square-foot multi-purpose arena is constructed of pre-cast concrete, masonry, and glass. The canopy that shades the entrance and enormous bay window is made up of 350 panes of glass.

Action on the Hardwood *(top)*

The Cleveland Cavaliers basketball team takes to the hardwood of Quicken Loans Arena. In addition to being home to the CAVS since 1994, the arena is home to the Lake Erie Monsters hockey team and hosts numerous sports and entertainment events. With an intimate 21,500-seat capacity, 60 percent of the seats are on the lower level. The arena also has a sports bar, restaurant, and a team shop.

The Prize *(bottom)*

During the NBA Finals, a large-scale replica of the silver NBA Finals Championship trophy was on display in front of Quicken Loans Arena. Though this work of art was temporary, the arena features a collection of public art, a first for a sports and entertainment facility.

Go Browns! *(top)*

The Cleveland Browns football team, founded
in 1946, takes to the field against the Detroit
Lions. The Browns play at Cleveland Browns
Stadium on one of the first heated natural
grass fields in the NFL to crowds of 73,200.

"Dawg Pound" *(bottom)*

The most dedicated and fun-loving fans of the
Cleveland Browns sit in the "Dawg Pound,"
a two-level 10,000 bench seating section on
the east side of Browns Stadium. In the same
location as in old Municipal Stadium, the
fans continue the tradition of wearing colorful, creative apparel while having a howling
good time.

Cleveland Browns Stadium

Fireworks erupt over Cleveland Browns Stadium. Constructed on the lakefront site of the old Municipal Stadium, the new structure opened in 1997 with the return of the Cleveland Browns and football. The stadium is built of concrete and steel with glass-enclosed staircases and elevator towers. A light-finished exterior creates openness while windscreens provide comfort to fans seated on the upper deck.

The Old Arcade *(opposite)*

The 1890 jewel on Euclid Avenue regained its luster in 2001 when developers renovated the national landmark. Light fixtures, intricate brass rails, golden oak woodwork, stone floors, and the sweeping stairs were all restored. Today, the Hyatt Regency Cleveland occupies the two towers and top three floors of the atrium while retail shops and a food court comprise the first two floors.

Renaissance Cleveland *(right and below)*

Opened in 1918 as the Hotel Cleveland, the Renaissance Cleveland, a Marriott, is part of the Tower City complex on Public Square. A charter member of Historic Hotels of America, the 12-story structure with interior atrium has 500 rooms offering luxurious modern amenities with rich historical elements, a 22,600 square-foot ballroom, exhibit space and Sans Souci, an elegant restaurant. The lobby, with vaulted ceilings and high arched windows, staircase, and signature Carrara marble cloverleaf fountain, has been renovated to retain its classical elegance.

The Galleria at Erieview *(above)*

Built in 1987 as a postmodern boutique mall at the base of the Tower at Erieview, the two-level, 200,000 square-foot Galleria features art galleries, boutiques, and restaurants. A three-segment barrel-vaulted skylight spans almost the entire public area. The East 9th Street façade features a glass and granite arched entrance.

Tower City Center *(opposite)*

In the heart of the city, Tower City Center is part of the Tower City Complex. The complex is comprised of the historic Terminal Tower and attached historic office structures, Sky-light Office Tower, Ritz-Carlton Hotel, rapid transit station, and multi-level shopping mall. The center was the city's main train station before being converted to a mall and continues to serve the East and West Sides of town with light rail service.

Peace Memorial Fountain

Reaching toward the heavens, *Peace* rises from the flames of conflict. The monumental work of bronze and polished granite by artist Marshall Fredericks was placed on Mall A in 1964.

Free Stamp *(opposite)*

Commissioned by the Standard Oil Company in 1982 to stand upright on a granite pad in front of their new Public Square headquarters, the Free Stamp was rejected when new owners, British Petroleum, took over the firm. The company donated the Claes Oldenburg/Coosje van Bruggen sculpture to the city. Located on the lawn east of City Hall, the sculpture rests on its side where it is the subject of much debate.

Honest Abe *(left)*

A large bronze and granite statue of Abraham Lincoln holding the Gettysburg Address stands in front of the Cleveland Board of Education building on East 6th Street. A gift of the school children of Greater Cleveland in 1932, the statue stands 12-feet high with the base. Engraved plaques around the base of the pedestal include the text of his famous address.

Soldiers and Sailors Monument *(right)*

The most visible monument in Cleveland is on the southeast quadrant of Public Square. Built in 1894, the Soldiers and Sailors Monument commemorates the battlefield heroes of Cuyahoga County during the Civil War. The names of 6,000 men are engraved in marble within the Memorial Room of the base chamber. The chamber is entered through ornate brass doors and contains relief panels depicting battles.

Monument to Victory *(above)*

Bronze sculptures on each of the four sides of the Soldiers and Sailors Monument represent the Infantry, Artillery, Cavalry, and the Navy. Sculptor/Architect Captain Levi T. Scofield designed the square building, which is set on top a sandstone esplanade. It has a 125-foot granite shaft that is capped with a 15-foot "Goddess of Liberty." A bronze eagle hovers over the north and south entrances.

Cleveland Fire Fighters Memorial *(opposite)*

Fire fighters are depicted facing the danger of fire in this contemporary memorial, which bears the names of 76 firefighters who have died in the line of duty since the department formed in 1862. Dedicated in 2003, it replaces an earlier 1965 memorial and was made possible by the Cleveland Fire Fighters Memorial Fund, comprised of current and retired Cleveland fire fighters.

On Stage at the Palace *(opposite, top)*

The auditorium in the grand Palace Theatre seats 3,680. Across the ceiling and over the proscenium arch are ivory and gold leaf while the marble is warmed with drapes of mulberry brocade and velvet. The large stage has seven stories of fly space for storage of curtains and backdrops. An orchestra pit was added during the 1980s restoration.

The Grand Hall *(opposite, bottom)*

Billed as, "The Most Beautiful Playhouse in the World" when it opened in 1922, the Palace Theatre retains its glamour. The Grand Hall of Neo-Classic design features walls, pillars and a floor of solid marble. Two marble staircases at each end sweep up the mezzanine where railings are of ornamental bronze from Germany. Five chandeliers of Czechoslovakian crystal, replicas of those at Versailles, grace the ceiling.

The Ohio Theatre *(above)*

The theatres of Playhouse Square, dark since 1969-70, faced demolition when a non-profit group, The Playhouse Square Foundation, was formed in 1973 to save them. A capital campaign fund drive made renovations possible. The Ohio Theatre had sustained substantial fire damage but was restored and reopened in 1982. The theatre often features famous touring musicals from the Broadway Series.

At the State *(top)*

The State Theatre at Playhouse Square hosts performers from string quartets to ballet and opera. For performers, a new stage house was designed with contemporary amenities while the rest of the theatre retains its traditional ambiance. Here, the Cavani String Quartet & Cleveland FES performs during the Ingenuity Festival of Art & Technology.

State Theatre Lobby *(bottom)*

Murals by artist James Dougherty titled, *The Spirit of Cinema in America*, encircle the lobby of Vermont marble and artistic wainscoting. Once considered the largest in the world, the lobby was completely restored and a concession stand added.

The Playhouse Square Historic District

The Cleveland Theater District is a thriving entertainment area thanks to vision and loving restoration. Patrons have a variety of theatrical and musical attractions to choose from in the State, Palace, Ohio, Allen, and Hanna theatres. Office buildings, stores, and restaurants complement the theaters while a 750-car parking garage serves the district.

The Great American Rib Cook-off
(opposite and above)

A Memorial Day weekend tradition, the Cook-off marks the unofficial beginning of Northeast Ohio's summer season. Barbecue masters from around the state, country, and the city gather to create mouth-watering ribs and other delicacies to sell and win prizes. Begun in 1992 and held at the Time-Warner Amphitheater, admission includes music from nationally-recognized performers.

Grand Prix of Cleveland *(above and left)*

Every summer there's a roar on the lake-front as "Indy" cars take to the course at Burke Lakefront Airport on the shores of Lake Erie. Since 1982, some of the greatest names in auto racing have taken the checkered flag. The three-day festival is headlined by the Champ Car World Series, North America and includes celebrity races, displays, music, and food for all ages.

Precision in the Sky *(opposite)*

The United States Air Force Thunderbirds precision flight team jets over the lakefront at the Cleveland National Air Show, a Cleveland tradition begun in 1929 as the National Air Races. On Labor Day weekend, aerobatics teams, wing-walkers, the U.S. Golden Knights parachute team, and the latest in armed forces aircraft take over the skies. For browsing, a static display of aircraft dating back to World War II, exhibits, and concessions are on the grounds of Burke Lakefront Airport.

The Crawford Auto-Aviation Museum *(above)*

The 1907 Model K touring car has been re-stored to its original condition and is one of less than a dozen known to exist. Crawford, part of the Western Reserve Historical Society in University Circle, houses one of the top automobile collections in the country. The collection illustrates the history of the automobile industry, nationally, and on the Western Reserve.

A Walk Through History *(opposite, top, left)*

First floor hallway of the Hay-McKinney house looking east into the reception hall. The house was designed by Abram Garfield, the son of martyred President James A. Garfield, for Mrs. John Hay, who replaced her Victorian mansion on Euclid Avenue with this Florentine-style villa.

Breakfast Room *(opposite, top, right)*

The Breakfast room and bow window, off the dining room of the Hay-McKinney house. The shield back American side chairs date from about 1800 and, although not original to the house, were typical of the emerging interest in American antiques in the first quarter of the twentieth century.

Museum Garden *(opposite, bottom)*

The garden of the Bingham-Hanna house was designed by the firm of Frederick Law Olmsted, the landscape planner who designed Central Park in New York. The fountain's bronze figure of a young girl is by noted American sculptor Harriet Frishmuth and is titled, *Playdays*.

Parade on the Circle

Over 50,000 spectators watch more than 1,000 participants perform while following a traditional parade route around Wade Park, Oval Drive, and East Boulevard in University Circle, the cultural crossroads of Cleveland. Begun in 1990 and held in June, the colorful community arts parade is presented by the Cleveland Museum of Art.

In Tall Order   *(left and right)*

Stilt-dancers are some of the performers in
Parade on the Circle. A community effort,
Cleveland artists, families, community
groups, and international and national artists
strut to Latin, jazz, reggae, funk, and techno
music.

Masked

Creativity rules at Parade on the Circle.
Provided with a theme, each participant
creates their own interpretation of it. For a
nominal entry fee, anyone can participate but
the costumes must be hand-made, and, no
written words, logos or motorized vehicles
(except wheelchairs) are allowed. In addition
to the parade, street performers, activities, and
concessions are located at Circle Village.

Children's Museum of Cleveland *(above)*

The only institution in Cleveland dedicated to the development of young children from birth to age eight, the Children's Museum offers exhibits and programs that enhance child development and family learning. Established in 1981 by parents, educators, and civic leaders, the museum was created as a "town square" where play inspires lifelong learning. The museum is located in the heart of University Circle, its tent-like roof a distinctive landmark.

Fun! *(left)*

Exhibits at the Children's Museum of Cleveland make learning fun. The water exhibit Splish! Splash!, featuring a two-story climbing structure, teaches children about water transportation and the earth's water structure. A House & Hospital exhibit has a two-story house and teaches real-life skills like housekeeping, shopping, banking, driving, and healthcare. Traveling exhibits add new experiences.

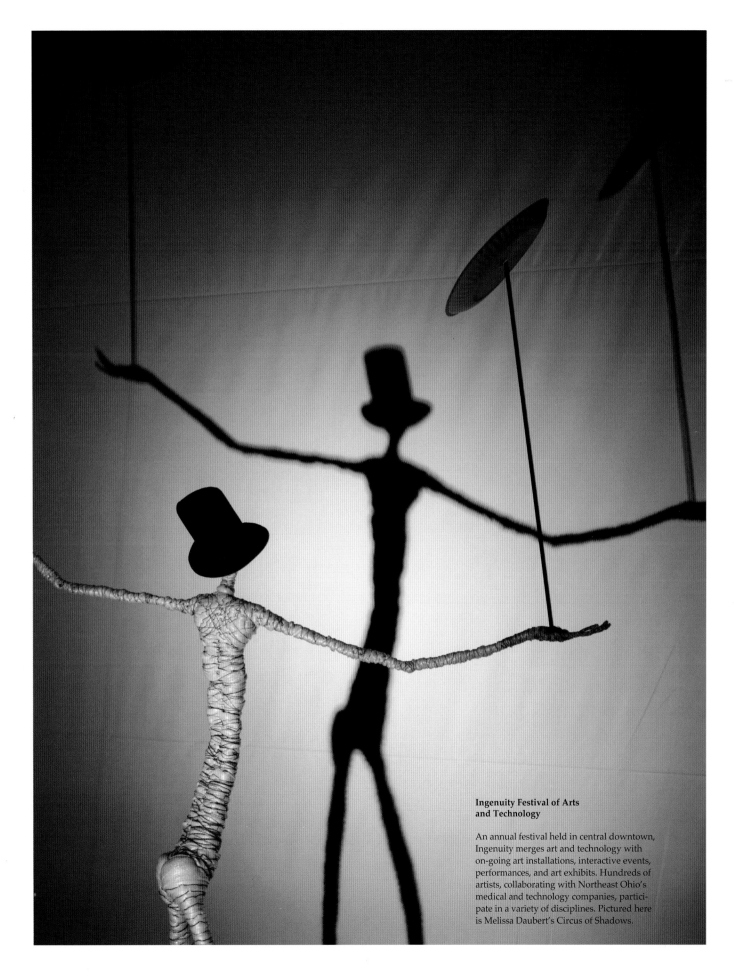

**Ingenuity Festival of Arts
and Technology**

An annual festival held in central downtown,
Ingenuity merges art and technology with
on-going art installations, interactive events,
performances, and art exhibits. Hundreds of
artists, collaborating with Northeast Ohio's
medical and technology companies, participate in a variety of disciplines. Pictured here
is Melissa Daubert's Circus of Shadows.

Echo Tube *(opposite)*

One of the more popular hands-on exhibits at the Great Lakes Science Center is the Echo Tube that educates about sound vibrations and echoes. The Science Center teaches all ages in the multiple disciplines of science using participatory exhibits.

The Great Lakes Science Center *(above)*

Constructed in 1996, the 165,000 square-foot building at the southwest corner of North Coast Harbor promotes the sciences through hands-on exhibits. Designed in an industrial/ technical style using concrete, metal and glass, it features a 320-seat OMNIMAX® theater inside a Monel metal-clad dome. As part of the center, the Steamship William G. Mather Museum is docked nearby.

MOCA *(above)*

The Museum of Contemporary Art (MOCA)
is a major exhibitor of provocative contemporary visual art and culture. Showcasing
national and international artists, as well as
established and emerging Cleveland area
talent, it is a major producer of traveling
exhibitions. One such exhibit is Side by Side, a
group exhibition of artists.

The Wade Park Lagoon *(opposite)*

Apple blossoms frame a springtime view of
the Neo-Classical Cleveland Museum of Art
in University Circle. The 300-foot long façade
of white Georgian marble features a central
Ionic-column portico. Opened in 1916, the
museum overlooks a terrace and formal
gardens as well as the lagoon.

NASA John H. Glenn Research Center and Visitor Center *(above)*

A panorama of scale model airplanes greets visitors in the lobby of the NASA Glenn Research Center's Visitor Center. The display graphically illustrates aeronautical and space progress past and present. Visitors can spend a day and enjoy an out-of-this-world inspirational experience. Located adjacent to Cleveland Hopkins International Airport, "NASA Glenn" was established in 1941 as one of three aeronautics centers nationwide.

Apollo Command Module *(left)*

Used during the Skylab 3 mission, the second manned mission to the first American space station, the module carried three astronauts to Skylab. The module is one of 6,000 square-feet of exhibits, including Aero-adventure, Flight Simulator, John Glenn Tribute, the Apollo Era, and the Solar System. The center also offers updates and communications on shuttle missions and the international space station.

Urban Fortress   *(above)*

Erected as a headquarters for the Cleveland Gray's, which was founded in 1837 as a private militia, the Romanesque Revival-style building of rusticated sandstone and brick is a museum and events center. The structure is four-stories high with a five-story tower. The main entry arch rests on polished granite columns. A black wrought-iron drop-gate forms a barrier between the front steps and the massive oak doors.

Gray's Lobby   *(right)*

A carved staircase that decorates the lobby of Gray's Armory features a museum of military artifacts, swords, guns, uniforms, and a cannon. The armory has hosted some of the city's major social events in its large stage hall, at one time the largest in town. The first Cleveland Auto Show was held in this space as were performances by the Metropolitan Opera.

Dunham Tavern Museum

Dunham Tavern Museum on Euclid Avenue
is the oldest building in Cleveland still stand-
ing on its original foundation. The clapboard
structure, constructed of heavy hewn timbers
joined by wooden pins and hand-wrought
spikes, was a tavern and stagecoach stop
along the Buffalo-Cleveland-Detroit Road. It
is now a public museum.

The Tap Room *(top)*

A game board with pieces that can be used for a variety of games, including chess are found in the Tap Room. On the windowsill are two pierced lanterns. A dried floral arrangement sits on the 18th century table bench.

Upper Hallway *(bottom)*

Two spinning wheels are on display at the Dunham Tavern Museum: a small flax wheel and a large wool wheel. In the back is a yarn winder called a weasel. Forty turns of the wheel measured out a skein of yarn. The popping sound emitted by the machine when that limit was reached is the origin of the expression "pop goes the weasel.".

Polar Bear Watching   *(above, left)*

A journey through Northern Trek, home to cold climate animals at the Cleveland Metroparks Zoo, can lead to an encounter with polar bears. The zoo's exhibit of bear species is one of the largest in North America. Founded in 1882, the zoo features thousands of animals in state-of-the-art natural habitats on 165-acres, including a children's farm.

Camel Ride   *(left)*

At the Cleveland Metroparks Zoo's Australian Adventure, opened in 2000, one can enjoy a camel ride, feed nectar to a lorikeet, watch a puppet or animal show, or hop on the Boomerang Express train for a ride to experience life "Down Under."

Rainforest Stroll   *(above)*

Explore the jungles of Asia, Africa, and the Americas inside the 87,000 square-foot Rain Forest building. Enclosed in reflective glass panels supported on an aluminum and steel frame with a soaring dome, the two-acre complex features more than 10,000 plants and 600 animals, including Bornean orangutans, ocelots, and free-flying birds. Highlights include a 25-foot waterfall and a simulated tropical rainstorm.

Cleveland Museum of Natural History
(opposite, top)

Greeting visitors at the front entrance is *Steggie*, a life-sized Stegosaurus sculpture created by Louis Paul Jonas in 1968. Founded in 1876 as the Kirtland Society of Natural Science, the museum moved to Wade Park Oval in University Circle in 1955 and has undergone several expansions. The museum has since added HealthSpace Cleveland and EcoCity Cleveland.

Sears Hall of Human Ecology   *(opposite, bottom)*

Watching wildlife is something humans have done since Prehistoric times. Sears Hall is dedicated to examining how humans interact with the natural world around them. Plants, animals, and artifacts from cultures from North and South America, Mesoamerica, Africa, Australia, and New Guinea are represented. The Museum's permanent exhibits and collections deal with ecology, evolution, dinosaurs, anthropology, cultures, insects, and more.

Dinosaurs   *(above)*

Children stand in awe of the mounted *Allosaurus fragilis*, "Alice," the 40-foot long, 15-foot tall meat eater that lived 160 million years ago. On display in the Kirtland Hall of Prehistoric Life in the Cleveland Museum of Natural History, it is part of a collection of over four-million specimens. The Museum, founded in 1920 and located in Wade Oval in University Circle, promotes research, education, and conservation.

Festival of Freedom *(opposite and above)*

Fireworks explode over the Conrail Bridge on the Cuyahoga River in the Flats. A July Fourth annual tradition, the festival features fireworks set to music and are visible from all over the city. The main vantage point is from Edgewater Park, part of Cleveland Lakefront State Park. Edgewater has 131 acres of open space, picnic grounds, and a 900-foot-long beach.

Cleveland Botanical Garden *(opposite, top)*

Featuring ten-acres of spectacular outdoor gardens, the garden was renovated and expanded in 2003, creating a new dramatic main double-door entrance. Added was the Eleanor Armstrong Smith Glass House, an 18,000 square-foot geometric glass conservatory featuring two unique ecosystems: the Spiny Desert of Madagascar and the Cloud Forest of Costa Rica. The two biomes have over 500 plant and 50 animal species.

Cloud Forest *(opposite, bottom)*

Inside the Glass House of the Cleveland Botanical Garden, a Costa Rican cloud forest is recreated complete with palms, black olive, fig, and avocado trees. Orchids and bromeliads thrive in the misty environment. Over 200 butterflies and exotic birds fly freely over a waterfall and gorge while visitors observe the tropical tree canopy from a 25-foot elevated walk.

Botanicals *(above)*

Stargazer lilies add color to a carpet of ferns at the Cleveland Botanical Garden where a variety of flora and fauna are on display in theme gardens.

Scenic Stroll

Stone paths lead through outdoor gardens at the
Cleveland Botanical Garden. Lush plants and
flowers can be viewed in the Japanese Garden,
Western Reserve Herb Society Garden, Wood-
land Garden, Mary Ann Sears Swetland Rose
Garden, Campsey-Stouffer Gateway Garden,
and the C.K. Patrick Perennial Garden. The
Hershey Children's Garden was the first public
children's garden in Ohio. Accessible to all is the
Elizabeth and Nona Evans Restorative Garden.

German Cultural Garden   *(left)*

The Cleveland Cultural Gardens were created as a commemorative project to recognize the contributions of ethnic groups in Cleveland. In the German Cultural Garden stands a statue of Johann Wolfgang von Goethe and Johann Christoph Freidrich von Schiller. Both men were 18th century poets and dramatists, Goethe the author of *Faust*.

Summertime in the Cultural Garden   *(right)*

A bronze bust by sculptor Frank J. Jirouch of Polish scientist Nicolaus Copernicus, considered the father of modern astronomy, graces the Polish Cultural Gardens. Established in 1926, the gardens in historic Rockefeller Park, with their lush landscaping, paved terraces, and commemorative sculpture create a quiet and reflective outdoor museum of ethnic diversity.

Brecksville Reservation

The 16 reservations of the Cleveland Metroparks consist of over 21,000 acres and are commonly referred to as the "Emerald Necklace" because the reservations encircle the city of Cleveland. Chippewa Creek in the northern section of Brecksville Reservation, flows through a gorge that was left behind by glaciers that once blanketed the area.

Whirlpools and Water Falls

Euclid Creek Reservation, part of the Cleveland Metroparks, is located in the eastern suburbs of Euclid, South Euclid, and Richmond Heights. Named after the meandering Euclid Creek which flows the length of the reservation, the area is known for bluestone, a blue-gray siltstone once quarried for sidewalks and construction.

Cattails on the Lake   *(above)*

Located in the Cuyahoga Valley National
Recreation Area, part of the Cuyahoga Valley
National Park, is the tranquil Sylvan Pond.
The park, stretching from Cuyahoga through
Summit counties, has 125 miles of hiking
trails. The Towpath Trail follows the Erie and
Ohio canals. Other highlights are Brandywine
Falls, the Cuyahoga Valley Scenic Railroad,
buildings, bridges, and lakes.

Hale Farm and Village   *(opposite, top)*

The bell tower of a country meeting house in
the recreated village of Wheatfleld, beckons
visitors to the 200-year-old Civil War era
working farm and educational center. Part
of the Western Reserve Historical Society,
Hale Farm features period crafts made on the
premises by skilled artisans demonstrating
glassblowing, blacksmithing, weaving, candle
making, and basket making.

Long and Winding Road   *(opposite, bottom)*

Under a canopy of autumn foliage, the
2.5 mile Euclid Creek Trail runs from the
Highland picnic area in Euclid to Green Road
in South Euclid. It cuts through the Euclid
Creek Reservation, part of the Cleveland
Metroparks, the oldest park district in Ohio.

The Nature Center at Shaker Lakes   *(above)*

Exploring nature inside and out is the goal at the Shaker Nature Center. Founded in 1966 as a result of a community effort to preserve the Shaker Parklands from development as a freeway connecting Cleveland's East side to downtown, the center has become a leader in preservation and nature education. The renovated center features community gathering space, meeting rooms, classrooms, a gift shop, an outdoor deck, and a nature experience area.

The Nature Center   *(opposite, top)*

In 2003, the Nature Center at Shaker Lakes was renovated and updated using sustainable building practices and materials to limit environmental impact, including the use of geothermal heating and cooling. Such concern for the environment is fitting since the Shaker Parklands were designated as natural green space for the citizens of Cleveland back in the 19th century.

Jean Eakin Bird Observation Station
(opposite, bottom)

Over 10,000 walkers, runners, and birders annually use the trails and grounds of the Shaker Nature Center for exercise and to commune with the natural world. In 1971, the National Park Service named the center a National Environmental Education Landmark, one of the first to be so recognized.

Peter B. Lewis Building

Named after the chief executive and president of Cleveland-based Progressive Insurance, Frank Gehry's architecture on the campus of Case Western Reserve University makes a statement. The undulating curves and shapes are said to symbolize the methods in which management and business are taught at the Weatherhead School of Management, which is based in the deconstructed-style building.

U.S.S. Cod *(above)*

One of the 236 fleet submarines built during World War II, the *Cod* had an illustrious career before being decommissioned in 1954, when it was towed to Cleveland to serve as a reserve training vessel. The *Cod* has been preserved as a floating memorial to the more than 3,900 submariners who lost their lives. The *Cod* is credited with sinking more than 12 enemy vessels, was awarded seven battle stars, and performed the only international submarine-to-submarine rescue in history.

Down the Hatch *(left)*

The U.S.S. *Cod* is the only U.S. submarine that has not had stairways or doors cut into her pressure hull for public access. Visitors use the same vertical ladders and hatches that were used by its crew.

Floating Landmark *(above)*

A hit with Cleveland school children, the U.S.S. *Cod* is one of the city's most popular tourist attractions. In 1986, the U.S. Department of the Interior designated the *Cod* a National Historic Landmark. Visitors roam the halls where ten officers and 70-71 enlisted men once served.

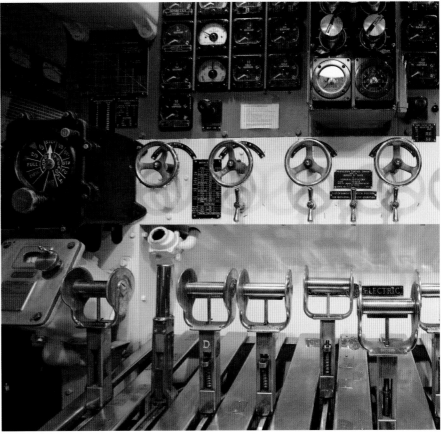

Full Speed Ahead *(right)*

Cleveland can claim partial credit as the U.S.S. *Cod*'s birthplace, since the submarine's four massive diesel engines were built by General Motor's Cleveland Diesel Plant on the West side. The Gatoclass diesel-electric submarine could travel at a speed of 20.25 knots surfaced and 8.75 knots submerged.

Steamship William G. Mather

Part of the Great Lakes Science Center and
docked at North Coast Harbor, the *William
G. Mather* was the flagship for the Cleveland-
Cliffs Iron Company. Named in honor of the
firm's then-President William Gwinn Mather
in 1925, it was the last ship owned by Cleve-
land-Cliffs, Inc. as it divested itself of Great
Lakes shipping interests. In 1987, the firm
donated the ship to be preserved as a museum
ship and floating maritime museum.

At The Wheel *(top)*

A classic straight-deck bulk carrier, the *William G. Mather* was the prototypical ore boat. The steamship incorporated the latest advancements and enhancements of its day, being the first to have radar installed and to have an automated boiler system. During its 55-year career, it carried millions of tons of iron ore, coal, grain, and distinguished guests. The *William G. Mather* was nick-named, "The Ship that Built Cleveland" because the city's steel mills were a frequent destination.

Captain's Quarters *(bottom)*

During the golden years of America's Great Lakes steamships, the *William G. Mather* was state-of-the-art in capacity, power, and accommodations. The steamboat was known for its elegant passenger's quarters.

Port of Cleveland

The city of Cleveland began shipping operations at the Port in 1825 and has continued to aid in the economic development of Northeast Ohio by keeping industries connected to the world. Since the opening of the Great Lakes and St. Laurence Seaway System in 1959, Cleveland is one of the premier ports in the system, supporting over 11,000 jobs.

Steel Making at Mittal Steel U.S.A.
(opposite, top)

Modern steel making converts molten steel to a coil of hot-rolled steel in a continuous process, using a twin-strand continuous slab caster, to create flat-rolled steel, which is supplied to the automotive, appliance, and electrical equipment industries. Mittal Steel U.S.A. is a fully integrated steel-making facilty.

Steel Town *(opposite, bottom)*

Since 1892, Ohio has been a leading steel producer and today, through the efforts of Mittal Steel U.S.A., remains among the top three steel-producing states. Here, oxygen is used to burn out steel build-up. Steel is the number one recycled material.

Mittal Steel U.S.A. *(above)*

Smoke rising from the blast furnace at Mittal Steel is a familiar sight in Cleveland and a reminder of the city's industrial past. Mittal is the largest steel producer in the nation and a major supplier to the North American automotive industry and other manufacturing sectors, and it operates some of the most modern and efficient steel plants.

111

Pouring of Molten Iron *(opposite)*

Molten iron of 2,900 degrees fahrenheit is being poured from a ladle into the Basic Oxygen Furnace at Steel Producing Shop #1-Mittal Steel U.S.A. - Cleveland, Inc., part of the dangerous process of making steel.

Dusk at the Veterans Memorial Bridge
(above)

Aglow in the evening, the Veterans Memorial Bridge, formerly known as the Detroit-Superior Bridge, crosses the Cuyahoga River, connecting the east and west sides of town. Opened in 1917, the bridge was designed to carry highway and streetcar traffic. This view is from the Stonebridge Condominiums.

Reflections

Reflected in the glass curtain wall of the contemporary Virgil E. Brown Cuyahoga County Child Support Enforcement Agency Building, is the spire of historic St. Peter's Church. The third church built in Cleveland and the oldest Catholic church in continuous service was founded in 1853 to serve German-speaking immigrants. In 1985, a joint ministry was formed with the Neuman Center at Cleveland State University, whose students bring new life to the parish.

The Red Line *(above)*

A Red Line rapid transit rail car zips out of the Ohio City station. Part of the Regional Transit Authority (RTA), the rapid line connects the East and West sides and airport with downtown and the waterfront. Begun in 1955, the light rail trains and buses replaced streetcars that had traversed the city. Cleveland was the first in the nation with a rail link connecting a downtown to an airport.

Ohio City *(left)*

From 1836 to 1854, the "City of Ohio" was its own independent community. In 1854, Ohio City was annexed to the city of Cleveland. Located on the Near West Side, across the Cuyahoga River, the area was originally populated by Germans, Hungarians, and Irish immigrants. In 1968, the Ohio City Redevelopment Association was created and transformed the area.

Home Sweet Home *(above)*

Lovingly restored century homes with committed owners have revitalized the Ohio City community, as seen here with this Queen Anne Victorian- style home. With the addition of new residential construction, antique stores, shops, offices and restaurants, a thriving neighborhood has been created with young professionals and over 15 ethnic groups sharing the 4.5 square-mile area.

Historic Tremont *(right)*

Tremont is one of Cleveland's oldest neighborhoods settled by immigrants. Set high on a bluff overlooking a bend in the Cuyahoga River, it features many historic churches and structures. Lemko Hall, once a saloon and residence, was a Slavic social club that was featured during the wedding reception scene in the film, *The Deer Hunter*. In 1987, it was converted into commercial space and condominiums.

West Pierhead Lighthouse *(above)*

The Cleveland Harbor West Pierhead Light-house, constructed in 1911, features a conical cast-iron tower incorporated into the keeper's quarters and was fitted with a fourth-order Fresnel lens. In 1916, the one and a half-story fog signal was added and called, the "cow" because of its sound, a signal to sailors as far out as 12 miles. In 1965 the lighthouse became automated and the lens donated to the Great Lakes Science Center.

Sails in The Sunset *(opposite)*

Sailboat racing is one watercraft activity enjoyed on Lake Erie. Edgewater Park, part of the Cleveland Lakefront State Park, is located on the west end of Lake Erie with recreational facilities, including the Edgewater Yacht Club and the Edgewater Marina.

Sunset Over Cleveland *(page 128)*

As the sun sets, another day of sights, sounds, and activities draws to a close.